EXPLORING PRAYER
WITH THOMAS MERTON

*Dedicated to
Philip Garwood*

Exploring Prayer
with Thomas Merton

*compiled and edited
by Tony Castle*

ST PAULS

Also in this series
(compiled and edited by Tony Castle)

Exploring Prayer with Pope John Paul II
ISBN 978-0-85439-741-9   48 pages   £2.99

Exploring Prayer with Blessed Charles de Foucauld
ISBN 978-0-85439-742-6   48 pages   £2.99

Exploring Prayer with St Thérèse of Lisieux
ISBN 978-0-85439-763-1   48 pages   £2.99

Photograph of Thomas Merton by John John Howard Griffin.
Used with permission of the Merton Legacy Trust and the
Thomas Merton Center at Bellarmine University.

ST PAULS Publishing
187 Battersea Bridge Road, London SW11 3AS, UK
www.stpaulspublishing.com

Copyright © ST PAULS, 2009
ISBN 978-0-85439-764-8

A catalogue record is available for this book from the British Library.

Set by Tukan DTP, Stubbington, Fareham, UK
Printed and bound in Great Britain by Athenaeum Press Ltd,
Gateshead, Tyne & Wear

ST PAULS is an activity of the priests and brothers
of the Society of St Paul who proclaim the Gospel
through the media of social communication

Contents

Introduction	7
Action Man of Prayer	9
The Spiritual Life	13
Our Calling	14
Union with Christ	15
A Life of Love	16
Radiating Divine Love	17
Recollection and Presence I	18
Recollection and Presence II	19
Recollection and Presence III	20
Meditative Prayer	21
Emptying Oneself	22
Resonance of Contemplation	23
Exploring the Inner Ground	24
Work as Prayer	25
Destiny of Love	26
The Path to Sanctity	27
A Prayer Corner	28
Praying Everywhere	29
A Child's Prayer	30

Simple Affective Prayer	31
Finding Love	32
Discovering an Old Unity	33
Action and Contemplation	34
Praying in the Spirit	35
Action of the Holy Spirit	36
Prayer from the Centre	37
Praying the Psalms	38
Psalms Full of Christ	39
Psalms: Best Praise of God	40
Why is Prayer Dead? I	41
Why is Prayer Dead? II	42
The Psalms Reveal God, 'our treasure'	43
Peace in the Will of God	44
All in the Psalms	45
Psalms: God's Words in Us	46
Mary and the Psalms	47
Sources	48

Introduction

Prayer is to the Christian what water is to the goldfish or air to the eagle. Without it there can be no Christian life. The essential nature of prayer can best be observed, and imitated, in the lives of those disciples of Jesus who have grown close to him in love. Their lives are totally centred upon and imbued by prayer, because the love of Christ and their neighbour informs everything that they are and everything that they do. Because they are human they are not without sin, but that vivid and daily realisation only serves to deepen their dependence upon and love for Christ, and thereby their prayer.

In this Exploring Prayer series the intention is not to provide a collection of the prayers of a saintly disciple of Christ – although there will be the occasional prayer which will encapsulate the direction of their spiritual life – but to explore some aspects of their life (a life informed and directed by prayer) and, more prominently, to consider some short reflective passages from their writings, bearing on prayer, which may assist us on our pilgrim way.

Thomas Merton was a contemplative monk and a writer who produced an immense literary output. His early writings presented monastic spirituality to the public; and it had a very wide appeal. Throughout his copious publications the central and unifying theme is prayer, and particularly contemplative prayer. No other modern writer has explored contemplation so widely and deeply. He recommends contemplative prayer to every Christian and describes it as an awareness or an awakening of man to the presence of God within him.

Action Man of Prayer

Thomas Merton 1915-1968

As Thomas Merton left New York, in December 1941, on the train bound for Kentucky and the Cistercian Abbey of Gethsemani, the news of Pearl Harbour and America's entry into the War was ringing in his ears. Should he pursue his desire to seek God in a hidden life of prayer and contemplation, he pondered, or should he now be volunteering for the Armed Forces? He decided that, at twenty-six, if he was rejected by the severe Cistercian Order (popularly known as Trappists)- as he had already been by the Franciscan Order – he would offer himself at the recruiting office. Fortunate for us and Western Christianity, he was offered a trial period at the Abbey.

Thomas became Brother Louis on 19 March 1944, when he took his first vows; and later Father Louis when he was ordained priest in 1949. So the professor of English, author and poet, who had lived a flamboyant, permissive life, like Charles de Foucauld and the great Augustine of Hippo, left the world behind and embraced the austerity of the Cistercian way of life. In one of his early books, *The Silent Life*, he explains that this 'austerity was not considered an end in itself but a means of putting off the 'old man', corrupted by sin'. In the monastery he experienced the love and sense of family that had eluded him in the world.

Born of artist parents, in France in 1915, his father was from New Zealand and his mother from the United States. Thomas did not know the warmth of normal family life and could never forget how, at the age of six, his mother told him, in a formal letter, of her approaching death! Ten years later his father also died. Later he wrote of the upheavals and sadness of his early years, in the internationally acclaimed *The Seven Storey Mountain* (1952); published in England as *Elected Silence*.

Merton was educated in England, at Oakham School and Clare College, Cambridge, moving on, before taking a degree, to Columbia University, New York. He took up a professorship in English at St Bonaventure's University, in the same city, and it was here that Thomas first encountered Franciscan friars and became exposed to Catholicism. His conversion had much to do with the influence of the writings of John Henry Newman and the convert Jesuit poet, Gerald Manley Hopkins.

While he was Brother or Father Louis to his community, to the public he was always Thomas Merton. Although he was ever obedient to his superiors, conflicts arose over the driving need he had to write. (He had over sixty-five books and pamphlets published.) Highly regarded and loved by his brothers in the community, for years he longed for greater solitude and in 1965 eventually obtained permission to live as a hermit in the Abbey grounds. From his hermitage poured out letters to presidents, world leaders and the Pope. His life of prayer overflowed in a compelling concern for world peace, the threat of nuclear extinction and the pollution of the environment. His abbot, in return, received countless letters of complaint about the guru in his garden, who dared to apply spiritual values to world issues!

In his *No Man Is an Island* (1967) Thomas wrote, 'Every other man is a piece of myself, for I am a part and a member of mankind. Every Christian is part of my own body, because we are members of Christ'. He really lived this belief and suffered deeply in trying to reconcile his love for monastic silence with the deep concerns thrown up by his life of prayer.

In his correspondence with the leaders of World Religions, Father Louis sought for a common, spiritual unity and he was particularly interested in Zen Buddhism. In 1968 he obtained permission to leave his monastery and travel to the East to address a conference in Bangkok. On the way he met the Dalai Lama and visited Sri Lanka. The story of his first real journey in twenty-seven years, which proved to be his last, is recorded in his *Asian Journal*.

He died shortly afterwards, in Thailand, on the twenty-seventh anniversary of his arrival at the gates of the Abbey of Gethsemani, electrocuted by a faulty shower.

The personal conflict Thomas Merton experienced in 1941, on the train bound for Kentucky, between the call to a life of prayer and a life of action, was wonderfully and painfully resolved.

By becoming a man of prayer and love he became irresistibly a great man of action for, as he says himself, 'action and prayer are fused into one entity by the love of God and of our brother in Christ'.

The Spiritual Life

'In life and death we depend entirely on him'

It is impossible to think about prayer without first enquiring, What is the Spiritual Life? It is the silence of our whole being in compunction and adoration before God, in the habitual realisation that he is everything and we are nothing, that he is the centre to which all things tend, and to whom all our actions must be directed. That our life and strength proceed from him, that both in life and death we depend entirely on him.

Thoughts in Solitude

Our Calling

'We must be ourselves by being Christ'

Every person is called to *be* someone. In order to be what we are meant to be, we must know Christ, and love him, and do what he did.

Our destiny is in our own hands, since God has placed it there and given us his grace to do the impossible. It remains for us to take up courageously and without hesitation the work he has given us, which is the task of living our own life as Christ would live it in us.

No Man Is an Island

Union with Christ

'The Holy Spirit makes us live by the love of God'

The Holy Spirit not only makes us understand something of God's love as it is manifested to us in Christ, but he also makes us live by the love of God and experience its action in our hearts. When we do so, the Spirit lets us know that this life and action are the life and action of Christ in us. And so the charity that is poured forth in our hearts by the Holy Spirit brings us into an intimate, experiential communion with Christ.

No Man Is an Island

A Life of Love

'All we have to do is to believe and to love'

What we are called to do is to live as habitually and constantly as possible, with great simplicity, on this level of love which proceeds from the depths of our own being where Christ reigns and loves.

This is a dimension of life which no one can take away unless we close the door ourselves and no one can bring it in unless we open the door to Christ, opening our hearts to Christ and dwelling there.

A Conference on Prayer (India) unpublished

Radiating Divine Love

'Living as true members of Christ'

Accepting God's love in faith implies the need to share both that love and that faith. If Christians living in the world are to live as true members of Christ and radiate the divine influence among the people with whom they are in contact, they will be obliged to develop rich interior lives of union with God, and this union will have to be deep enough to weather the demands of hard work and constant contact with things that would defile a weaker spirit.

The White Pebble

Recollection and Presence I

'Recollection makes us present to ourselves, and to God'

Recollection should be seen not as an absence, but as a presence. It makes us present to ourselves; it makes us present to whatever reality is most significant in the moment of time in which we are living. And it makes us present to God and brings his presence to us.

No Man Is an Island

Recollection and Presence II

*'Prayer confesses our absolute dependence
on the Lord of life and death'*

Prayer means yearning for the simple presence of God, for a personal understanding of his word, for knowledge of his will and for a capacity to hear and obey him.

It is thus something much more than uttering petitions for good things external to our deepest concerns or repetitious praise.

All true prayer somehow confesses our absolute dependence on the Lord of life and death. It is a deep and vital contact with him whom we know not only as Lord but as Father.

The Climate of Monastic Prayer

Recollection and Presence III

'Recollection makes us present to God'

Recollection makes us present to God, and to ourselves in him. It is true that we are always present to God who sees all and keeps all things in existence but we are more present to him when we are aware of his nearness to us. For then the presence is conscious and mutual; it is the presence of a person to a person. And it is only when we are thus present to him that we truly discover ourselves as we really are.

No Man Is an Island

Meditative Prayer

'Meditation is a meeting with someone whom we already possess'

In meditative prayer one thinks and speaks not only with one's mind and lips, but in a certain sense with one's whole being. Prayer is then not just a formula of words, or a series of desires springing up in the heart – it is the orientation of our whole body, mind and spirit to God in silence, attention and adoration. All good meditative prayer is a conversion of our entire self to God.

Thoughts in Solitude

Emptying Oneself

*'A person must empty himself and give himself
to other people'*

A person cannot enter into the deepest centre of himself and pass through that centre into God, unless he is able to pass entirely out of himself and empty himself and give himself to other people, in the purity of a selfless love.

New Seeds of Contemplation

Resonance of Contemplation

'We become God's echo and his answer'

Contemplation is the response to a call: a call from him who has no voice, and yet who speaks in everything that is, and who, most of all, speaks in the depth of our own being: for we ourselves are words of his. But we are words that are supposed to respond to him, to answer him, to echo him, and even in some way to contain him and signify him. Contemplation is this echo. It is a deep resonance in the inmost centre of our spirit in which our very life loses its separate voice and re-sounds with the majesty and the mercy of the Hidden and Living One.

New Seeds of Contemplation

Exploring the Inner Ground

*'A disciplined experience is necessary
for fruitful action'*

When I speak of contemplation, I am talking about a special dimension of inner discipline and experience, a certain integrity and fullness of personal development, which are not compatible with a purely external, alienated, busy-busy existence.

Without a more profound human understanding derived from exploration of the inner ground of human existence, love will tend to be superficial and deceptive. Traditionally the ideas of prayer, meditation and contemplation have been associated with this deepening of one's personal life and this expansion of the capacity to understand and serve others.

Contemplation in a World of Action

Work as Prayer

'My work can purify and pacify my mind and dispose me to prayer'

The requirement of work to be done can be understood as the will of God. If I am supposed to hoe the garden, or lay the table, then I will be obeying God if I am true to the task I am performing. To do the work carefully and well, with love and respect for the nature of the task and with due attention, is to unite myself to God's will in my work. In this way I become his instrument. He works through me. When I act as his instrument my work cannot become an obstacle to prayer.

New Seeds of Contemplation

Destiny of Love

'If we love God we discover ourselves in him'

We are what we love. If we love God, in whose image we were created, we discover ourselves in him and we cannot help being happy: we have already achieved something of the fullness of being for which we were destined in our creation. If we love everything else but God, we contradict the image born in our very essence, and we cannot help being unhappy, because we are living a caricature of what we are meant to be.

The Waters of Siloe

The Path to Sanctity

'The joy of God is everywhere'

Be content that you are not yet a saint, even though you realise that the only thing worth living for is sanctity. Then you will be satisfied to let God lead you to sanctity by paths that you cannot understand. You will travel in darkness in which you will no longer compare yourself to others. Those who have gone by that way have finally found out that sanctity is in everything and that God is all around them, they suddenly wake up and find that the joy of God is everywhere.

New Seeds of Contemplation

A Prayer Corner

'Let there be a place where your mind can be idle and worship the Father in secret'

There should be at least a room, or some corner where no one will find you and disturb you or notice you. You should be able to untether yourself from the world and set yourself free, loosing all the fine strings and strands of tension that bind you, by sight, by sound, by thought, to the presence of other people.

Once you have found such a place, be content with it, and do not be disturbed if a good reason takes you out of it. Love it, and return to it as soon as you can, and do not be quick to change it for another.

New Seeds of Contemplation

Praying Everywhere

'Know how to meditate when you are waiting for a bus'

Learn how to meditate on paper. Drawing and writing are forms of meditation.

Learn how to contemplate works of art.

Learn how to pray in the streets or in the country.

Know how to meditate not only when you have a book in your hand, but when you are waiting for a bus or riding in the train.

Above all, enter into the liturgy and make the liturgical cycle a part of your life – let its rhythm work its way into your body and soul.

New Seeds of Contemplation

A Child's Prayer

'There is not a child's prayer uttered that does not sing hymns to God'

There is not a flower that opens, not a seed that falls into the ground, and not an ear of wheat that nods on the end of its stalk in the wind, that does not preach and proclaim the greatness and mercy of God to the world. There is not an act of kindness or generosity, not an act of sacrifice done, or a word of peace and gentleness spoken, not a child's prayer uttered, that does not sing hymns to God.

The Seven Storey Mountain

Simple Affective Prayer

*'It is possible to live consciously in
an atmosphere of prayer'*

It is clear that those who have progressed a certain distance in the interior life not only do not need to make systematic meditations, but rather profit by abandoning them in favour of a simple and peaceful affective prayer, without fuss, without voice, without much speech, and with no more than one or two favourite ideas or mysteries, to which they return in a more or less general and indistinct manner each time they pray.

New Seeds of Contemplation

Finding Love

*'To find love
I must enter into the mystery of God'*

To say that I am made in the image of God is to say that love is the reason for my existence, for God is love. Love is my true identity. Selflessness is my true self. Love is my true character. Love is my name.

If, therefore, I do anything or think anything or say anything or know anything that is not purely for the love of God, it cannot give me peace, or rest, or fulfilment, or joy. To find love I must enter into the sanctuary where it is hidden, which is the mystery of God.

New Seeds of Contemplation

Discovering an Old Unity

'The deepest level of communication is communion'

The deepest level of communication is not communication, but communion. It is wordless. It is beyond words, and it is beyond speech, and it is beyond concept. Not that we discover a new unity. We discover an older unity. We are already one. But we imagine that we are not. And what we have to recover is our original unity. What we have to be is what we are.

The Asian Journal

Action and Contemplation

'Action and prayer for the true Christian are inseparable'

Action and contemplation for the true Christian are inseparable. Far from being essentially opposed to each other, interior contemplation and external activity are two aspects of the same love of God. Action is love looking outward to other people, and contemplation is love drawn inward to its own divine source. Action is the stream, and contemplation is the spring. The spring remains more important than the stream, for the only thing that really matters is for love to spring up inexhaustibly from the infinite abyss of Christ and of God.

No Man Is an Island

Praying in the Spirit

'Prayer transforms our vision of the world'

If we pray 'in the Spirit' we are certainly not running away from life, negating visible reality in order to 'see God'. For the Spirit of the Lord has filled the whole earth. Prayer does not blind us to the world, but it transforms our vision of the world, and makes us see it, mankind and the history of mankind, in the light of God.

To pray 'in spirit and in truth' enables us to enter into contact with that infinite love, that inscrutable freedom which is at work behind the complexities and the intricacies of human existence.

Contemplative Prayer

Action of the Holy Spirit

*'This life and action
are the life and action of Christ in us'*

The Holy Spirit... not only makes us understand something of God's love as it is manifested to us in Christ, but he also makes us live by that love and experience its action in our hearts. When we do so, the Spirit lets us know that this life and action are the life and action of Christ in us. And so the love that is poured forth in our hearts by the Holy Spirit brings us into an intimate, experiential communion with Christ.

No Man Is an Island

Prayer from the Centre

'Awakening the profoundest depths of our being in the presence of God'

We rarely pray with the 'mind' alone. Monastic meditation, prayer, *oratio*, contemplation, and reading involve the whole person, and proceed from the centre of a person's being, his 'heart' renewed in the Holy Spirit, totally submissive to the grace of Christ. Monastic prayer begins not so much with 'considerations' as with a 'return to the heart', finding one's deepest centre, awakening the profoundest depths of our being in the presence of God who is the source of our being and our life.

The Climate of Monastic Prayer

Praying the Psalms

'In the Psalms we drink divine praise at its purest and stainless source'

Does the Church love the Psalms merely because they are ancient and venerable religious poems ? The Church indeed loves what is old, not because it is old but rather because it is 'young'. In the Psalms we drink divine praise at its pure and stainless source, in all its primitive sincerity and perfection. We return to the youthful strength and directness with which the ancient psalmists voiced their adoration of the God of Israel. Their adoration was intensified by the ineffable accents of new discovery: for the Psalms are the songs of men who knew who God was. If we are to pray well we too must discover the Lord to whom we speak.

Praying the Psalms

Psalms Full of Christ

'The Psalms are full of the Incarnate Word'

The reason why the Church loves the Psalms is because God has given himself to her in them, as though in a sacrament.

The Psalms are full of the Incarnate Word. Not only is David a 'type' of Christ, but the whole Psalter has always been regarded by the Church, in her liturgy, as though it were a summary and compendium of all that God has revealed. In other words the Psalms contain in themselves all the Old and New Testaments, the whole Mystery of Christ. In singing the Psalms each day, the Church is therefore singing the wedding hymn of her union with God in Christ.

Praying the Psalms

Psalms: Best Praise of God

'The Psalms are the best possible way of praising God'

It is by singing the Psalms, by meditating on them, loving them, using them in all the incidents of our spiritual life, that we enable ourselves to enter more deeply into that active participation in the liturgy which is the key to the deepest and truest interior life. If we really come to know and love the Psalms, we will enter into the Church's own experience of divine things. We will begin to know God as we ought. And that is why the Church believes the Psalms are the best possible way of praising God.

Praying the Psalms

Why is Prayer Dead? I

'Praise is now so overdone everyone is sick of it!'

Do we really know what it means to praise? To adore? To give glory?

Praise is cheap today. Everything is praised. Soap, beer, toothpaste, clothing, film stars – everything is constantly being praised. Praise is now so overdone that everybody is sick of it, and since everything is 'praised' with the official hollow enthusiasm of the radio presenter, it turns out in the end that *nothing* is praised. Praise has become empty.

Are there any superlatives left for God? There is no word left to express our adoration of him who alone is Holy, who alone is Lord.

Praying the Psalms

Why is Prayer Dead? II

'We do not really think we need God'

So we go to God to ask for help and to get out of being punished, and to mumble that we need a better job, more money, more of the things that are praised in the advertisements. And we wonder why our prayer is so often dead – borrowing its only urgency from the fact that we need these things so badly. But we do not really think we need God. Least of all do we think we need to praise him. If we have no real interest in praising him, it shows that we have never realised who he is.

When one becomes conscious of who God really is, and when one realises that he who is Almighty, infinitely Holy and has 'done great things for us', the only reaction is the cry that bursts from the depth of our being in amazement at the tremendous goodness of God to human beings.

Praying the Psalms

The Psalms Reveal God, 'our treasure'

'The function of the Psalms is to reveal God as the "treasure"'

The Psalms not only form our minds according to the mind of the Church, not only direct our thoughts and affections to God, but they *establish us in God*, they unite us to him in Christ. But they do this only if our hearts follow their thoughts and words back into the inspired source from which they have come to us. Therefore the sentiments of the Psalmist, which are the thoughts and sentiments of God himself in his Church, must lead us into the hidden sanctuary of God. Where our treasure is, there will our hearts be also. The function of the Psalms is to reveal to us God as the 'treasure'.

Praying the Psalms

Peace in the Will of God

'There is not one of us who does not seek peace'

If there is one theme that is certainly to be found in all the Psalms, it is the *motif* of Psalm One. 'Blessed is anyone who rejects the advice of the wicked... but who delights in the law of the Lord.' If there is one 'experience' to which the Psalms all lead in one way or another, it is precisely this: delight in the law of the Lord, *the peace in the will of God*. This is the foundation on which the Psalmists build their edifice of praise.

There is therefore one fundamental religious experience which the Psalms can all teach us: *the peace that comes from submission to God's will and from perfect confidence in him.*

Praying the Psalms

All in the Psalms

'We only have to take advantage of the texts and use them with faith, confidence and love'

There is no aspect of the interior life, no kind of religious experience, no spiritual need of man, that is not depicted and lived out in the Psalms. But we cannot lay hands on these riches unless we are willing to work for them. It is not so much a matter of study, since the study has been done for us by experts. We need only to take advantage of the texts they have given us, and use them with faith, and confidence and love. Above all we need zeal and strength and perseverance. We cannot by mere human ingenuity or talent exhaust all that is contained in the Psalms.

Praying the Psalms

Psalms: God's Words in Us

'Let God pray in us in his own words'

If we only seek to get something out of them, we will get less than we expect, and generous efforts may be frustrated because they are turned in the wrong direction: towards ourselves rather than toward God.

In the last analysis, it is not so much what we get out of the Psalms that rewards us, as what we put into them. If we really make them our prayer, really prefer them to other methods and expedients, in order to let God pray in us in his own words, and if we sincerely desire above all to offer him this particularly pure homage of our Christian faith, then indeed we will enter into the meaning of the Psalms.

Praying the Psalms

Mary and the Psalms

'Mary understood the Psalms as no one else could'

The sanctity of the most holy Mother of God, who is our model as well as our most powerful protector in the life of grace, was nourished and increased by her love for these inspired texts. Mary understood the Psalms as no one else could understand them: she meditated on them constantly, keeping all their words and pondering them in her heart.

Her *Magnificat* sprang from the depths of her soul and gives us a kind of synthesis and summary of all the poetry of the Old Testament. With her as our guide and teacher, we will easily come to love the Psalms and to appreciate their hidden beauty.

Praying the Psalms

SOURCES

A Conference on Prayer (India) quoted by John J. Higgins SJ, in Thomas Merton on Prayer, Doubleday & Co., New York, 1973

Contemplation in a World of Action, by Thomas Merton, Doubleday & Co., New York, 1971

Contemplative Prayer by Thomas Merton, Herder & Herder, New York, 1969

New Seeds of Contemplation by Thomas Merton, New Directions, Norfolk, Conn. USA, 1961

No Man Is an Island by Thomas Merton, Image Books New York, 1967

Praying the Psalms by Thomas Merton, Liturgical Press, Collegeville, Minnesota, 1956

The Asian Journal by Thomas Merton, ed. Noami Burton, New Directions, New York, 1968

The Climate of Monastic Prayer by Thomas Merton, article in *Collectanea Cisterciensium* vol.27, 1965

The Seven Storey Mountain by Thomas Merton, Signet Books, New York, 1952

The Waters of Siloe by Thomas Merton, Image Books, New York, 1962

The White Pebble by Thomas Merton, article in 'Sign' July 1950 issue.

Thomas Merton on Prayer by John J. Higgins SJ, Doubleday & Co. New York, 1973

Thoughts in Solitude by Thomas Merton, Image Books New York, 1968